ECONOMIC ISSUES 8

Why Is China Growing So Fast?

Zuliu Hu
and
Mohsin S. Khan

INTERNATIONAL MONETARY FUND
WASHINGTON, D.C.

ISBN: 1-55775-641-4
ISSN: 1020-5098

Published April 1997

To order IMF publications, please contact:

International Monetary Fund, Publication Services
700 19th Street, N.W., Washington, D.C. 20431, U.S.A.
Tel.: (202) 623-7430 Telefax: (202) 623-7201
Internet: publications@imf.org

Preface

The Economic Issues series aims to make available to a broad readership of nonspecialists some of the economic research being produced in the International Monetary Fund on topical issues. The raw material of the series is drawn mainly from IMF Working Papers, technical papers produced by Fund staff members and visiting scholars, as well as from policy-related research papers. This material is refined for the general readership by editing and partial redrafting.

The following paper draws on material originally contained in IMF Working Paper 96/75, "Why Is China Growing So Fast?" by Zuliu Hu and Mohsin S. Khan of the IMF's Research Department. Rozlyn Coleman prepared the present version. Readers interested in the original Working Paper may purchase a copy from IMF Publication Services ($7.00).

Why Is China Growing So Fast?

In 1978, after years of state control of all productive assets, the government of China embarked on a major program of economic reform. In an effort to awaken a dormant economic giant, it encouraged the formation of rural enterprises and private businesses, liberalized foreign trade and investment, relaxed state control over some prices, and invested in industrial production and the education of its workforce. By nearly all accounts, the strategy has worked spectacularly.

While pre-1978 China had seen annual growth of 6 percent a year (with some painful ups and downs along the way), post-1978 China saw average real growth of more than 9 percent a year with fewer and less painful ups and downs. In several peak years, the economy grew more than 13 percent. Per capita income has nearly quadrupled in the last 15 years, and a few analysts are even predicting that the Chinese economy will be larger than that of the United States in about 20 years. Such growth compares very favorably to that of the "Asian tigers"—Hong Kong, Korea, Singapore, and Taiwan Province of China—which, as a group, had an average growth rate of 7–8 percent over the last 15 years.

Curious about why China has done so well, an IMF research team recently examined the sources of that nation's growth and arrived at a surprising conclusion. Although capital accumulation—the growth in the country's stock of capital assets, such as new factories, manufacturing machinery, and communications systems—was important, as were the number of Chinese workers, a sharp, sustained increase in productivity (that is, increased worker efficiency) was the driving force behind the economic boom. During 1979–94 productivity gains accounted for more than 42 percent of China's growth and by the early 1990s had overtaken capital as the most significant source of that growth. This marks a departure from the traditional view of development in which capital investment takes the lead. This jump in productivity originated in the economic reforms begun in 1978.

Measuring Growth

Economists studying China face thorny theoretical and empirical issues, mostly deriving from the country's years of central planning and strict government control of many industries, which tend to distort prices and misallocate resources. In addition, since the Chinese national accounting system differs from the systems used in most Western nations, it is difficult to derive internationally comparable data on the Chinese economy. Figures for Chinese economic growth consequently vary depending on how an analyst decides to account for them.

Although economists have many ways of explaining—or modeling—economic growth, a common approach is the neoclassical framework, which describes how productive factors such as capital and labor combine to generate output and which offers analytical simplicity and a well-developed methodology. Although commonly applied to market economies, the neoclassical model has also been used to analyze command economies. It is an appropriate first step in looking at the Chinese economy and yields useful "benchmark" estimates for future research. The framework does, however, have some limitations in the Chinese context.

Original data for the new IMF research came from material released from the State Statistical Bureau of China and other government agencies. Problematically, the component statistics used to compile the Chinese gross national product (GNP) have been kept only since 1978; before that, Chinese central planners worked under the concept of gross social output (GSO), which excluded many segments of the economy counted under GNP. Fortunately, China also compiled an intermediate output series called national income, which lies somewhere between GNP and GSO and is available from 1952 to 1993. After making appropriate adjustments to the national income statistics, including adjusting for indirect business taxes, these data can be used to analyze the sources of Chinese economic growth.

A Surprising Find

Much previous research on economic development has suggested a significant role for capital investment in economic growth, and a sizable portion of China's recent growth is in fact attributable to capital investment that has made the country more productive. In other words, new machinery, better technology, and more investment in infrastructure have helped to raise output. Yet, although the capital stock grew by nearly 7 percent a year over 1979–94, the capital-output ratio has hardly budged. In other words, despite a huge expenditure of capital, production of goods and services per unit of capital remained about the same. This pronounced lack of capital deepening suggests a constrained role for capital. The labor input—an abundant resource in China—also saw its relative weight in the economy decline. Thus, while capital formation alone accounted for over 65 percent of pre-1978 growth, with labor adding another 17 percent, together they accounted for only 58 percent of the post-1978 boom, a slide of almost 25 percentage points. Productivity increases made up the rest.

It turns out that it is higher productivity that has performed this newest economic miracle in Asia. Chinese productivity increased at an annual rate of 3.9 percent during 1979–94, compared with 1.1 percent during 1953–78. By the early 1990s, productivity's share of output growth exceeded 50 percent, while the share contributed by capital formation fell below 33 percent. Such explosive growth in productivity is remarkable—the U.S. productivity growth rate averaged 0.4 percent during 1960–89—and enviable, since productivity-led growth is more likely to be sustained. Analysis of the pre- and post-1978 periods indicates that the market-oriented reforms undertaken by China were critical in creating this productivity boom.

The reforms raised economic efficiency by introducing profit incentives to rural collective enterprises (which are owned by local government but are guided by market principles), family farms, small private businesses, and foreign investors and traders. They also freed many enterprises from constant intervention by state authorities. As a result, between 1978 and 1992, the output of state-owned enterprises declined from 56 percent of national output to 40 percent, while the share of collective enterprises rose from 42 to 50 percent and that of private businesses and joint ventures rose from 2 to 10 percent. The profit incentives appear to have had a further positive effect in the private capital market, as factory owners and small producers eager to increase profits (they could keep more of them) devoted more and more of their firms' own revenues to improving business performance.

China's recent productivity performance is remarkable. By comparison, productivity growth for the Asian tigers hovered around 2 percent, sometimes slightly more, for the 1966–91 period. China's rate of almost 4 percent simply puts it in a class by itself.

Why the Productivity Boom?

Exactly how did China's economic reforms work to boost productivity, especially in an economy still burdened by extensive government controls? In the important rural sector the story is particularly interesting.

Prior to the 1978 reforms, nearly four in five Chinese worked in agriculture; by 1994, only one in two did. Reforms expanded property rights in the countryside and touched off a race to form small nonagricultural businesses in rural areas. Decollectivization and higher prices for agricultural products also led to more productive (family) farms and more efficient use of labor. Together these forces induced many workers to move out of agriculture. The resulting rapid growth of village enterprises has drawn tens of millions of people from traditional agriculture into higher-value-added manufacturing.

Further, the post-1978 reforms granted greater autonomy to enterprise managers. They became more free to set their own production goals, sell some products in the private market at competitive prices, grant bonuses to good workers and fire bad ones, and retain some portion of the firm's earnings for future investment. The reforms also gave greater room for private ownership of production, and these privately held businesses created jobs, developed much-wanted consumer products, earned important hard currency through foreign trade, paid state taxes, and gave the national economy a flexibility and resiliency that it did not have before.

By welcoming foreign investment, China's open-door policy has added power to the economic transformation. Cumulative foreign direct investment, negligible before 1978, reached nearly US$100 billion in 1994; annual inflows increased from less than 1 percent of total fixed investment in 1979 to 18 percent in 1994. This foreign money has built factories, created jobs, linked China to international markets, and led to important transfers of technology. These trends are especially apparent in the more than one dozen open coastal areas where foreign investors enjoy tax advantages. In addition, economic liberalization has boosted exports—which rose 19 percent a year during 1981–94. Strong export growth, in turn, appears to have fueled productivity growth in domestic industries.

In one final area, price reform, the Chinese have proceeded cautiously, granting a fair amount of autonomy to producers of consumer goods and agricultural products but much less to other sectors. Several bouts of inflation have buffeted the Chinese economy in the past two decades, deterring the government from implementing full-scale price liberalization. High rates of growth also raise inflationary worries. Inflation may pose the single greatest threat to Chinese growth, though thus far it has been largely contained.

A More In-Depth Look

As with any national economy, China has unique characteristics that the researcher must properly account for.

First, many researchers cite the periodic political crises that seized China before 1978 as a factor obscuring pre-1978 economic strength. Because the political climate in China was so much in flux, these commentators argue, the economic pictures before and after 1978 cannot be compared with any accuracy. This proposition was evaluated by dropping from the analysis the 1958–70 subperiod, which encompasses the Great Leap Forward and the Cultural Revolution. The result is that pre-1978 productivity increased only modestly as a result, from 1.1 to 1.6 percent.

Second, in the 1953–78 period Chinese central planners invested heavily in the urban industrial sector and restricted migration from the country into the cities. Could the abandonment of this policy after 1978 itself explain the strong performance of the economy? Did these sectoral shifts drive growth, or did productivity? In the event, although these sectoral shifts are important, they do not eliminate the independent rise in productivity associated with the reforms.

Third, some commentators maintain that if the productivity growth was a one-time shot of adrenaline to the body economic, it is certainly not sustainable. In fact, productivity gains have been steady throughout 1979–94 and even increased during 1990–94. If the post-reform period is broken into three distinct phases, each associated with a different set of reforms, sizable productivity gains are evident in each subperiod. This indicates that the Chinese were able to carry over initial productivity gains to other parts of the economy.

Finally, one can scrutinize the analysis for measurement problems. In particular, are the capital-stock data calculated properly and were there any measurement errors relating to the input data? Regarding the capital-stock measurement, since the Chinese national income statistics exclude the value of residential housing and since outlays for new housing rose during 1978–94, the investment figures should be adjusted accordingly. When this is done, there is no change to the pre-1978 productivity growth estimate and a modest increase in the post-reform productivity growth rate, which corroborates the general story. Could an overvaluation of the initial capital stock have biased the findings? More conservative estimates of the capital stock were used to re-analyze the data, but there is no strong evidence to refute the findings. Although the pre-1978 productivity gains become negative, the post-reform productivity rate is unaffected.

Another more significant problem with capital-stock data is that Chinese asset surveys do not produce capital stock estimates consistent with the investment data in the national accounts. The difficulties of bridging this statistical gap are considerable. The analytical findings of this study were compared with those obtained by economists who had computed the data somewhat differently. On the productivity side, the studies differed in emphasis but not in essence: as a body, the available evidence corroborates productivity improvements as a significant source of post-1978 growth, even when divergent capital-stock calculations are employed. The outside estimates of productivity growth vary from about 2 percent to nearly 4 percent for the 1979–94 period.

Regarding other input data, a study was made of the potential for a differential bias that might overstate the post-reform growth relative to the pre-reform period. This problem might arise because centrally planned economies are prone to the overreporting of output and the underestimating of prices. As it happens, although enterprise managers have traditionally tended to overreport output in an effort to meet production targets set by the government, the incentives to do so have probably declined in the reform era as managers have faced less strict state control. It is unlikely, therefore, that performance in the post-1978 era has been overstated relative to earlier eras.

The underdeflating of nominal output could be a more serious source of bias. The piecemeal character of price reform—with some sectors liberalized and others not—means that selecting an appropriate deflator for the post-1978 period is difficult. Yet, the central planning period may also have seen an underdeflation of output, since repressed inflation was probably widespread (as manifested in shortages, black market trading, and long waits for certain goods). Thus, the measurement problem, while real, probably does not much alter the basic conclusion about substantial productivity gains after 1978.

Conclusion

Although China occupies a unique niche in the world's political economy—its vast populace and large physical size alone mark it as a powerful global presence—it is still possible to look at the Chinese experience and draw some general lessons for other developing countries. Most important, while capital investment is crucial to growth, it becomes even more potent when accompanied by market-oriented reforms that introduce profit incentives to rural enterprises and small private businesses. That combination can unleash a productivity boom that will propel aggregate growth. For countries with a large segment of the population underemployed in agriculture, the Chinese example may be particularly instructive. By encouraging the growth of rural enterprises and not focusing exclusively on the urban industrial sector, China has successfully moved millions of workers off farms and into factories without creating an urban crisis. Finally, China's open-door policy has spurred foreign direct investment in the country, creating still more jobs and linking the Chinese economy with international markets.

China's strong productivity growth, spurred by the 1978 market-oriented reforms, is the leading cause of China's unprecedented economic performance. Despite significant obstacles relating to the measurement of economic variables in China, these findings hold up after various tests for robustness. As such, they offer an excellent jumping-off point for future research on the potential roles for productivity measures in other developing countries.

The Economic Issues Series

1. *Growth in East Asia: What We Can and What We Cannot Infer.* Michael Sarel. 1996.
2. *Does the Exchange Rate Regime Matter for Inflation and Growth?* Atish R. Ghosh, Anne-Marie Gulde, Jonathan D. Ostry, and Holger Wolf. 1996.
3. *Confronting Budget Deficits.* 1996.
4. *Fiscal Reforms That Work.* C. John McDermott and Robert F. Wescott. 1996.
5. *Transformations to Open Market Operations: Developing Economies and Emerging Markets.* Stephen H. Axilrod. 1996.
6. *Why Worry About Corruption?* Paolo Mauro. 1997.
7. *Sterilizing Capital Inflows.* Jang-Yung Lee. 1997.
8. *Why Is China Growing So Fast?* Zuliu Hu and Mohsin S. Khan. 1997.